# Having The Courage To Be In A Healthy Relationship

## Positive Thinking

E.J. Luy

Bloomington, IN  Milton Keynes, UK

authorHOUSE®

*AuthorHouse™*
*1663 Liberty Drive, Suite 200*
*Bloomington, IN 47403*
*www.authorhouse.com*
*Phone: 1-800-839-8640*

*AuthorHouse™ UK Ltd.*
*500 Avebury Boulevard*
*Central Milton Keynes, MK9 2BE*
*www.authorhouse.co.uk*
*Phone: 08001974150*

*First published by AuthorHouse 10/23/2006*

*ISBN: 1-4259-5864-8 (sc)*

*Library of Congress Control Number: 2006908882*

*Printed in the United States of America
Bloomington, Indiana*

*This book is printed on acid-free paper.*

# *Contents*

# 1.

## *Defining*
## *The Perfect Mate*

Looking back to when I was twelve years old, I wanted to picture myself being in a perfect relationship. It is amazing how I thought about relationships at a very young age. Of course, growing up in a broken family did not help much either, so I promised myself that one day, I would find myself my soul mate, and I would make it work, no matter what. So my journey began. I did not quite understand why some couples looked happier than others. So that always intrigued me. As I got older, I asked myself, how do you make a relationship work? Is it based on trial and error, or is it just that men and women are totally different species. It took me a long time to understand relationship issues. I have heard about the need to compromise, such as the woman being a surrender wife. Some of the earlier studies even suggest that couples just hold things in, to avoid any conflicts. So I asked myself, does one way work better than the others? As much as I wanted to experiment with what works and what does not, I was not ready to jump in and follow any of these suggestions and jeopardize my existing relationship.

I started to question everything. Am I willing to be a surrender wife? Does my partner like someone like that? What if my partner wants an independent woman who knows what she wants and does not have to give herself up to satisfy him? As you can see, a relationship is harder than what most experts tend to believe. A relationship takes time to build, just like any career you choose. Sometimes you are lucky to find your ideal job, and other times, it just does not work out. However, it is harder to replace a relationship, especially the ones that you want to stay in, despite some problems. You may want to leave, but you may feel stuck in your current relationship. If there was an easy solution to unravel bad relationships, there would not be many couples spending time in a therapist's office or in the courtroom. By far, I do want to believe that most couples will try to resolve the issues they have in their relationships, rather than just giving up the moment an issue arises. So why do some couples make it and many others don't? Successful couples who have made it through their golden years have always fascinated me. I am always intrigued to ask those who have made it for so many years, feeling that they must carry a secret. This has always fascinated me as a child, as I came to grasp the failing marriage of my parents. I did not want to be like them, and I wanted to prove to everyone I could find that "perfect" mate. I did not want my parents' bad marriage to become my history as well. So as I discovered failed relationships many times, I was starting to wonder if there was such a thing as a "perfect" relationship.

# 2.

## *Men And Women Having Different Roles*

Since the existence of man and woman, the man has always been identified as the hunter and the woman as the gatherer. However, things have changed since then. But does this change the way men and women want to connect with each other? I truly believe that it has not. Women still want to be protected, and men want to be the protector. When these two systems collide, there is bound to be a potential conflict. When a woman no longer feels protected, she will be in doubt of her man. When the man feels that his efforts have not been acknowledged, he will feel rejected. So, even recognizing this as a potential problem, can something be done? After all, we cannot change the way one thinks. I feel that a relationship goes deeper than that.

What do you say to a couple who stays together for the sake of companionship? Are they happy or are they just satisfying their loneliness? I know so many couples who stay together for the sake of companionship. They look happy to me. Is it true that as people get older, they seem to want to stay for the sake of having somebody? It is totally understandable to be with someone rather than being alone and lonely, right? What price are we going to pay for happiness, or is this for selfish reasons? We cannot judge who is happy just by looking at couples. Couples can look happy, but they can be having problems. Some don't look happy, but are satisfied in their relationships. Simply put, we just cannot judge the book by its cover.

# 3.

I grew up in a broken family, so the meaning of a healthy relationship and finding an ideal mate was not embedded in me. Experts agree that those who grew up in a broken family, especially those who have experienced childhood abuse, will oftentimes become victims of abuse or grow up abusing others. Women who are victims of domestic violence oftentimes have an abused history or have witnessed the abuse between their parents. So, does having a perfect relationship correlate with someone's childhood experience? Most experts probably agree. However, we also know that this does not always happen. There are those who grew up being abused as a child, who have overcome the abuse, and who are in a perfectly healthy relationship. Yet, it's been known time and time again that people who come from an abusive childhood or broken family have a higher incidence of being in an abusive situation than those who come from a healthy and solid family. It is also true that some people have managed to be resilient. I learned how to be resilient at a young age, when both my mother and father left me. My father abandoned me, and my mother decided to better her life in America. By dealing with your past, you will learn to move on. Until then, this extra baggage you carry on your shoulders will likely make it to your next relationship.

We cannot rule out the possibility that people's experiences growing up with positive adults around them or even attaining a higher education can improve their lifestyles, including the chance of a healthy relationship. I did not have the right role model growing up, and if I neglected getting an education, my chance of ever finding a healthy relationship would be remote and small. It is true that you learn what has been passed down to you, and if you know nothing but dysfunctional relationships from your past, then this is all you know.

# 4.

<u>*Proving It*</u>

What about compatibility tests to prove how suited you are to your potential partner? There is not enough study done to show that this works. It may help you decide if you are compatible, but some couples are reluctant to disclose their flaws from the start. After all, couples tend to hide their worst traits until later on in the relationship. Then, it is often too late to turn back, as couples get comfortable with each other. I always enjoy watching dating shows, as couples try to break the ice. This proves that early dating takes a lot of energy, but it amazes me that some get the same connections right away. I do believe that some are in it for the wrong reasons. I believe that you just cannot measure something within you such as love, so I do find some credibility issues with most dating shows. One couple's definition of a satisfying relationship may be totally different from another couple's.

I do believe that you cannot prove love by some tests. It is within you, and you will know it when the right time comes. If you keep failing in your relationship, then you need to re-examine if what you are feeling is really love. You probably have a different perception what love is, and you need to find out within you if this love is a healthy one or a toxic one. When people close to you are telling you to get out of your relationship, but you keep on insisting he or she will change, it is time to really question yourself if what you are feeling is love or addiction.

# 5.

*For The*
*Right Reasons*

I learned that being with someone you are compatible with does not necessarily mean that it will work. I thought that having the same education, income, and family background were all necessary to be in a perfect relationship, but I realized that this was not always necessary. I believed this for so long, that I ended up in a wrong relationship every time. We all know that sharing the same traits or background is not always possible or necessary in order to be with someone you care about. I do believe that to be in a relationship, people need to accept who they are, and they do not lose themselves in the process. Let's try to remember Adam and Eve. Adam was in need of a companion, so Eve was created. Is relationship all about companionship then? I believe that it is more.

I think that no matter who you are, the important thing is you are satisfied where your relationship is heading. After all, relationship is a lot more complicated than most people think. I know some couples who are in a relationship to satisfy their own selfish needs and not in it for the right reason. It is never a good idea to rush your relationship. If you do, you end up battling it in divorce court. This takes a tremendous amount of energy, and you lose respect for yourself. There is just too much emotion when you rush yourself in your relationship, especially marriage. Not surprisingly, couples who do rush their relationships end up in a courtroom facing legal battles. It is also unfortunate that if they do have children, their children will too suffer. It is not surprising the divorce rate in Western society is so much higher than in countries that do not legalize divorce. It is also important to consider that where divorce is legal, this may also influence married couples to seek divorce, more than in a society that does not legalize divorce. It is common to hear that marriages end in less than a year, when it is legally within their rights to do so.

# 6.

## *Learning From Your Mistakes*

You see, relationships take many forms, whether you are in a heterosexual or homosexual partnership. What about individuals who decided not to be involved? Are they missing out being in a relationship? Again, being in a relationship does not mean you need to be with a romantic partner. I believe that friends, families, and other significant people in one's life constitute having a good relationship, and you do not necessarily need a romantic partner. I believe that if one is satisfied with that role, then the person does not need to seek out a partner to make the person complete. If a person depends on a partner for happiness, happiness can never be achieved. We all agree that money is not the key to happiness, but good health and families are far more important. Most people lose themselves in the process of finding a good partner when they have no faith in themselves.

I made the mistake of trying to please my partner to prove that I could make the relationship last. You are on a wrong path if you think that the relationship is never going to end. Again, it takes time to know your partner. You should not be afraid to admit that you have made a mistake after what you thought was an ideal relationship. People can only find the true meaning of a relationship after they make a mistake. If you remain in a relationship that is going nowhere, you are missing out in trying to find that ideal mate. I am not encouraging you to give up your existing relationship if you think it is worth saving. I am talking about a relationship that is beyond repairable. I spent four years in a relationship because I did not want to admit my failures without knowing the real meaning of a healthy relationship. In every relationship, there is something to be learned, and you should never think you wasted your time.

# 7.

## *Be Honest*

Many believe that couples who communicate better with each other have greater satisfaction in their relationship. It is proven time and time again that couples who are honest and do not hide their true selves have a greater chance of making their relationship last longer. Does this mean that couples need advice from professionals to improve their communication? This may be worth trying, if you and your partner agree to do so. You need to tell your partner how you are feeling, and you need to be truthful. Many problems arise when you hold things in. If you have something to say to your partner, then say it. You cannot expect your partner to read your mind. It is also true that no matter how hard couples try to make their relationship work, if one wants out, there is nothing the other one can do. Couples who do stay together for the sake of their children or for the sake of companionship tend to be unhappy in their marriage. If the couple decides to stay together, then maybe the marriage is more for convenience than anything else. Again, this brings us to the notion about the real reason why couples get married in the first place. We all know that love is the primary reason couples tie the knot, or is this notion of love no longer required when one is married? There are many factors that come into play once couples get married and they start having children. There may be financial reasons or emotional issues that come into play. So it is very important that people do try to find that right person early on in the relationship, before it becomes much more complicated later on.

# 8.

## *Be Yourself*

This brings us to the notion that not only do relationships take various forms, but also relationships are very complicated. Let's take Romeo and Juliet, for example. The end was tragic and indeed unfortunate. Does this mean that one will do anything for the sake of love? This seems to be true when we look at Shakespeare's love notion of Romeo and Juliet. But is this just the thinking of an imaginative writer? Perhaps. It is safe to say that a relationship is a complex matter, regardless how we try to make sense of it. Relationships go back centuries, but it still remains such an intriguing phenomenon. We are mesmerized by Hollywood marriages and who is connecting with whom. We want to see a perfect couple and are only to be disappointed when we find out later on that the perfect Hollywood couple did not survive after all.

What is it that makes it so glamorous and capturing? I believe that we don't want to admit we are deserving of finding that right person. We make up excuses that we have to be beautiful to be deserving of a right person. You have to admit your own vulnerabilities in order to accept yourself. It is the key ingredient in a satisfying relationship. If you are full of insecurities, you are an easy target for someone. You have to know yourself and what you want in a relationship to help you find that "right" person.

# 9.

## *Introspection*

A relationship can be very good in the beginning, then one starts to think if it is worth it to stay at the end. You see, we all have experienced happy times in our lives; unfortunately, we also suffer losses. But does this mean we give up hope of finding the secret to a happy relationship? Probably not. We need to be reminded that there is hope at the end of the tunnel and that one will find happiness within. *We all know that to love someone, we need to love ourselves first.*

It is also important to point out the power of religion or spirituality in our lives. It does not matter what your belief system is. We all need to be comforted by something greater than ourselves. We all need to know that we are not in control of our lives until we trust the power of a higher source. It is important for people to know that when they discover that, they will find inner peace within themselves. We also know that meditation helps a great deal in resolving conflict and anxiety within ourselves. It provides us with tranquility, peace, and solidarity.

# 10.

## *True Meanings*

A secret to a happy relationship may well just be a reflection of an ideal relationship that we all longed for. There may be couples out there who have found their ideal mate, thus considered this a success, and found a secret to maintain the excitement, loyalty, friendship, and all other things that we all want in a happy relationship. We must admit that this is rare; nonetheless, it is comforting to know that these relationships exist in this day and age. Can a fifty-year-old marriage have the same intensity as a couple who just got married? This may be true for some couples. This varies by definition of intensity. We all know that couples tend to relax after many years of marriage. The honeymoon stage, such as the flowers, candies, and movies seem to fall downward with most couples. Does this mean that many of these couples are no longer happy? It is obvious that the answer to this is of course not! A relationship is more than giving flowers, candies, and so forth... We now know that it is more complicated than that and it requires much more in-depth analysis.

# 11.

## _To Tolerate or Not_

When you ask your closest married friends to define their relationship, you are bound to get different responses. Someone once told me that a relationship was about compromise and tolerance for one another. I thought about that for a while and it made sense to me. Another friend of mine told me that her husband had forgotten to give her a birthday present, but she was not unhappy because she was becoming more tolerant of her husband's behavior. So, does this mean that she is happy? Possibly. You all know that you have a certain level of tolerance when it comes to those closest to you. You tend to be more forgiving than you are with a stranger. What makes my friend happy is different from yours or my happiness. It seems that tolerance does build up, the longer the relationship goes on. You must also be careful that your tolerance does not lead to anger, or you start blaming your partner. Again, assumptions can lead to many problems and you should start asking yourself whether your partner's behavior is making you unhappy. Oftentimes, we try not to tell our partner about what makes us angry, so we avoid addressing it. However, the more things get built up, the harder it is to get some resolutions.

# 12.

## *Staying or Leaving*

You also know of many couples who departed after many years of marriage, especially the ones whom you thought appeared very happy and content in their relationships. You start asking yourself, what would make someone do that? I know of a couple who was happy in their marriage, only to find out later on that there were keeping secrets in their relationship. Having secrets is always detrimental to a relationship. You need to confront yourself why you are not living true to yourself, or you will always feel uneasy about your relationship. You also know of many couples who stay in their marriage for the sake of saving it or because of their children, although it is clear they are unhappy. So does this mean that the secret of a long-lasting relationship is to sacrifice one's happiness or one's priorities? This may be true to some couples. It is important to understand that if this makes a person satisfied, this may unlock the secret to a happy relationship. However, this may just be an illusion. It is never easy to make a decision about your relationship. When there are emotions involved, the harder it is to set your mind in the different direction. It is crucial that you spend time alone and really try to understand if this person makes you happy. You have to ask yourself, is this what you want in ten or twenty years, and you should have an idea where you want this relationship to go.

# 13.

## *Finding Time*

I have heard from many couples who are so comfortable with each other that they sometimes don't notice their partner anymore. When asked if they are still happy in their relationships, they usually respond that they have not thought about it. Can this be the cause of the high divorce rate? You simply cannot live together by not noticing your partner anymore. You should find time to be alone together, to get to know each other again. It is amazing how couples forget about what makes the other person happy. One thing that is probably missing from most couples who are so used to each other is spontaneity and excitement. However, it is important to keep this alive. The issue of infidelity becomes a reality when one partner becomes bored or if he or she feels abandoned. This is never an excuse to have an affair, but it is important for couples to stay connected and bring the intensity back into their relationship.

When couples get too relaxed, they tend to forget what brought them together. It is only when things go wrong that the issues of boredom or lack of excitement in the relationship get brought up. Again, assuming that your partner is happy because you don't want to address his or her needs could lead to more problems.

# 14.

## *Avoidance*

The signs are usually obvious when a relationship goes sour. One couple told me that they just stopped talking. Another couple said that they just avoided each other by working too much or doing anything in order not to be with the person. We know that there are probably many more scenarios. As pointed out earlier, couples oftentimes become more tolerant of each other, so the idea of breaking off the relationship gets compromised with "putting up with his or her bad habits." This is not a healthy way to deal with your relationship that is in turmoil. Avoiding it does not resolve the issue, and you continue to escape your partner at all possible costs. You start living your lives as a separate person. You might work third shift so that you don't have to share the same bed. You are no longer a couple. This is a sad way to live your life.

Avoidance never leads to a resolution. It is easier to face your issues now, rather than looking back twenty years from now at what you could have done differently. You end up wasting so many precious years that you could have been spending in finding someone else. You are likely get emotionally drained from being in a bad relationship for so many years that by the time you are ready to move on, you are exhausted. This leads to many physical symptoms, as well as other emotional issues.

# 15.

## *Don't Fear Spirituality*

We have discussed many reasons why couples separate, and not so much what makes a happy couple. Again, this can take different forms, depending what a person's definition of happiness is. However, let's be practical. The main point of a happy couple consists of commitment, forgiveness, unselfishness, and most of all love for each other. We cannot dismiss how spirituality plays an important role in a couple's relationship. Some seek a higher power greater than themselves in helping them get through difficult relationships. I am not saying this is the same with someone who is coping with a terminal illness, but the perspective is similar. Let's look at a person who has survived cancer. If spirituality plays a big part of the person's coping skill, it is safe to say that it certainly needs to be looked at, and we have to consider it. In a committed relationship, you have to understand your partner's spirituality, and you need to try to be open to it. I am not saying you have to become spiritual yourself, but try to understand your partner's world of spirituality.

# 16.

## *There Are No Guarantees*

We all know of somebody who has had many failed relationships. There is no doubt that if we ask that person why it failed, we will get many responses. Is it true that one learns from their past relationship, and that the next relationship would be more of a success? What if the person has been married many times? Does that mean that he or she just can't find that right person? I think that we can learn from our past relationships to help us look at qualities we want in our next partner. This may improve the chance of finding that ideal relationship, but by no means can this guarantee happiness. You have to determine if your standards are too high or you are just not lucky in getting it right. Don't be afraid to admit your mistakes and move on. There is no sense in staying if it is really not working out. I rushed in with many of my relationships, and that's one thing I regretted. Knowing the person before you rush into things can save you time later on. It is harder to break the relationship when things get too serious. You also have to face your families and peers every time a relationship goes sour. Regardless how everyone else feels, however, you need to know what you want early on.

# 17.

*Dealing
With Emotions*

It may also be true that as couples become more tolerant of each other, they dismiss little things that would have been a big deal during the early phase of the relationship. Does this mean that they are satisfied or happy with their relationship? Again, not all relationships are perfect, by any means. What's more important are trust, love, and most of all happiness, even during the toughest times. Many couples will have disagreements from time to time.

When couples separate, their emotions play a big role. This means that there is a lot of baggage when couples decide to split. Some are able to reach an agreement, while others struggle with who should get the expensive piece of china. A relationship starts with lots of emotions and it normally ends that way as well. When we are dealing with emotions, it is hard to put perspectives in proper places, especially when couples are only concerned who gets the expensive china or who gets custody of the children. It is important that couples fight fairly and they do it respectfully.

# 18.

## *Accepting*
## *The Differences*

Let's talk about differences. Many times, couples split because of differences. I used to explain to my friends that my ex and I split because we were just too different. Let's look at this in a broader context. Being different should strengthen the couple more so than it should break the relationship. So, just because your partner likes to fix old junky cars does not mean that you should bicker with him or her about it. After all, you knew that prior to getting into the relationship and you should not expect your partner to change just because you don't like his or her hobbies. Who knows, maybe he or she will step into something that potentially would be a money-making hobby. Some people don't want to be involved because they know that their true identities may become nonexistent. Some may give up their dream of getting an education or whatever that interests that may be.

Couples will have better chance of success when they allow themselves to dream and not have their partner dictate their identity. After all, everyone reaches for a different dream, and no one should tell you otherwise.

# 19.

## *We Are Not Perfect*

Some couples may say that they are just simply bored of each other and that there are no surprises left in their relationship. Does this mean that one should terminate the relationship? One should try to find out what's important in that relationship, or doing some introspection. It is not unusual for couples to be bored after a while, but this comfort level should not be mistaken that one falls out of love. It is not surprising that at this level of commitment, one may stray and make a mistake. After all, we are only human. Again, it is important to catch this first sign of a problem than to fix it later. It is also not uncommon that most couples try to work things out, even after a betrayal. That is hard for anyone, since the trust that has been built for so long may never be regained. Some may ask if someone can ever forgive such a betrayal. The common phrase, "You will never understand until you are in my shoes" best fits this scenario. We sometimes forget that this can happen to anyone. We easily criticize famous politicians or celebrities when an affair gets public, not keeping in mind that famous or not, it can happen to you. So, why forgive? Again, it may be for a variety of reasons, such as financial, religion, children, or the fear of losing a longtime companion.

# 20.

## *What Is Right For You?*

So, does this mean that being in a relationship creates more problems than not being in one? I truly believe that finding that right person is the key to a successful relationship. Is there a right person? *My point here is the right person for you, not anyone else's idea of a right person.* It is true that being in a relationship takes time to build trust, comfort level, and commitment. Don't you want to invest this in the right person? Remember that when you say yes to the person, you are saying yes to a lifetime commitment, assuming this was your intention. As you and your mate become one, you bring two lives together, and this means that whatever your strengths and weaknesses are, you need to invest all your energy in this person. It is love that brought you and your mate joys to each other, and maybe having children together. As the couple unites, it is not uncommon that you hear someone say to you, "Love one another and may your life be filled with joys and children." So, not only is it yours and your mate's lifetime together, you are also responsible for the lives of your children, if you decide to have them and to give them an upbringing full of love that you and your mate once shared and continue to share from here on. The question whether you want to invest in finding the right partner for you is worth it, I am certain your answer is yes to this question.

# 21.

## *Facing The In-laws*

Let's not forget that when you decide to be in a committed relationship, you also have to face your in-laws. Let's say that you feel that the person is perfect for you, but you don't like his or her family members. So, does this mean that you are just going to end this relationship? It would be foolish to do so. This is not an uncommon problem when you may have a different background, race, and education. Instead, respect each other's differences and you will find that you can learn from each other's differences. You should never assume that they will accept you right away, nor you will like them right away. Remember, it is hard enough to get to know your future spouse until much later on in a relationship, much less getting to know your future spouse's family. I guess I like to point out that it can be overwhelming being in a committed relationship, and whether it is you or your partner needing to adjust, one should pay close attention to everyone's feelings and be respectful of that.

# 22.

## *Commitment*

I would like to go back to the issue of commitment. After all, this is why you are seeking the ideal mate or your perfect mate. There is a notion that men don't propose, for fear of <u>commitment.</u> Is this true? Or does this apply to women as well? In fairness, I believe that whether you are the woman or the man in the relationship, you must be ready to commit to your partner if you want to tie the knot. Men and women are different in the level of commitment, but I believe that we all want to be in an ideal relationship. Commitment means that you trust your partner and you accept each other for good times as well as bad times. It is also worth noting that when one's commitment is greater than the other, this causes turmoil in the relationship. Again, watch for subtle signs if your partner is not happy, and do something about it. If you and your partner don't have the same vibes, maybe it is time to look deeper into your relationship. *Don't be afraid to ask for help* if necessary. Maybe relationships end because of extra baggage you or your partner refuse to get help, thus you bring this into your relationship. The fear of commitment, for example, may be traced from your own upbringing, when you watched your parents' relationship sour. It may be as simple as having a bad partner, and this creates fear of pursuing your ideal mate.

# 23.

## _Confronting Yourself_

For some, it seems that luck is on their sides, or they are fortunate enough to find their ideal mate. But for many, it takes many failed relationships or marriages to finally find their soul mate. I had many failed relationships along the way, before I finally realized that I was going on the wrong path. I was too preoccupied with having a "right partner" to accept me. After many years of self-doubts, I was able to confront my imperfections. The biggest lesson I learned was to admit my imperfections and to be true to myself. Once I was able to accept this, I married my longtime true partner, and we now have a daughter. I wish I did not have to go through what I did, but in the end, it was an invaluable lesson. For others, accepting your true self may be easier said than done. If you have the emotional support of your family, this will help your healing process. If not, it is necessary to seek professional help if you keep on going down the wrong path. I cannot emphasize enough that to be a better person, you have to accept yourself. This means to let go of your past and your anger. Anger can sabotage many relationships. It also leads to many health issues such as an increase in your blood pressure, anxiety, and depression.

# 24.

## *Finding Strengths*

The secret of a happy relationship varies depending who you ask. For some, it may be financial stability and for others, it is for emotional reasons. Although you may struggle financially, you stay because your partner satisfies your emotional needs. To make my point, if you are happy with your partner for a right reason, than you have the skills in making your relationship last. A relationship is about partnership and trying to help your partner to be the best he or she can be. This means that you don't break a relationship because your partner is not making the amount of money that you have expected. I believe anyone can make a relationship work when the couple concentrates more on being a team rather than blaming the other. Lastly, asking for help or advice to make your relationship stronger is never a sign of weakness, but a sign of strength. You need to remember that you have the strength to make your relationship work if you really want it to. It is important to focus on your partner's strength, rather than what your partner is not doing. You need to utilize each other's strength to help you face many obstacles and problems that you both will encounter as long as you are both in a committed relationship.

# 25.

*Saying Sorry*

No matter how angry you are with your partner, it is never a good idea not to express it. Again, communication is important in any relationship. It is also wise to say you are sorry. I learned that if you admit you are sorry, it goes a long way. It is amazing how simple the word *sorry* is, but it makes a very significant impact.

When one is angry, it takes a lot of energy, and at the end, it is very exhausting. Instead of waiting another day, it is a good idea to resolve the issues as they arise. This saves a lot of hurt and anger. It is sometimes better to take a cool-off period if necessary, but the more you prolong the anger, the harder it is on your body. Many times, we want to win, and we stay mad as long as possible in order to win. In the past, I thought a silent treatment was needed, but this is

51

another way of avoiding the issue. Many couples have their ways of dealing with things, but having the right communication is the key.

Taking ownership of your mistakes can make your life much easier. I am learning a lot from my two-year-old daughter about how to be more patient. The days I feel angry, I do tell her I am sorry. It is true that no matter how little she is, she is a human being. We are all human beings and we all make mistakes. For this reason, by acknowledging our mistakes, we are telling others that we are human beings as well. It is easy to be angry and blame it on our partner. However, the longer one holds in the anger, the more build-ups occur. When I meet someone who has survived decades of marriage, I always ask how the person has made it that long. I am amazed how simple the response is. It is never go to bed angry, and tell your partner you are sorry. You see, it is that easy and it does not take a lot of energy to do.

# 26.

## *Assumptions*

We tend to assume a lot when it comes to relationships, especially when emotions come into play, but assumptions can lead to many problems, such as trust issues. To be with someone, you must have a strong trust of your partner. Many relationships suffer because one loses trust of the other. If trust has been compromised, it is harder to make your relationship work. You cannot just be filled with doubts that will make you want to interrogate your partner every time he or she is late from coming home. If you cannot trust your partner anymore, it may be time to really do a lot of serious thinking as to why. Assumptions lead to distrust, and it takes control of your relationship. You have to analyze why you are distrustful. Are you unhappy in your relationship? This may be a sign that you start to lose trust in your partner. I would like to give an example of something I learned in the past. I can honestly say that I almost lost my spouse who I care very deeply about, because of my own insecurities, and I made many mistakes in the process during our courtship. Luckily, we decided to rebuild our relationship. I am guilty of assuming things without merits. I don't want you to make the same mistake I once made. If you need time to figure out about yourself, you need to find that time. *You deserve to be happy.*

# 27

## *Facing Reality*

Finding the right person is never too late, no matter how old you are. When you make a mistake, learn from it and move on. Remember, you are in control of your own destiny, and it only makes sense that you invest in it wisely, in finding that right person for you. You should always know that in life, things do not go the way we want it to. You do have to accept the reality you may never find that right person. If you are lucky to have found your life partner, you must also understand that you can lose that at any time. In life, we have to deal with losses, so it is important that you never expect perfection or you will end up with disappointment. On the other hand, do not take your partner for granted. You need to show your partner that you appreciate him or her. Remember, you may not have that chance until it is too late. To have a fulfilling relationship is a joint effort, and how you learn from your past relationships can benefit your next relationship. Most of all, be happy for who you are in life by surrounding yourself with the right people and being in touch with your whole self.

# 28.

*Acceptance*

Acceptance is crucial in any relationship. Couples not only learn to tolerate each other, but are also accepting of their partner's weaknesses. You need to accept your partner's imperfections. When one enters the union of marriage or decides to live together, one finds some little annoyance about their partner. This little annoyance does get bigger when it is not resolved in a timely manner. We must remember that we cannot change our partner, but we learn to adjust to their imperfections. Couples sometimes forget that their partner's bad habits did not just happen overnight, and it will take time to change those habits. If your partner likes to squeeze the top of the toothpaste instead of the bottom, you have to learn to adjust to this habit. It is a longtime habit and it will take time to change that. If the issue is so insignificant, it does not make sense to even dwell on this.

When we enter into a more committed relationship, having to accept small imperfections should be expected. Again, when we expect too much of our partner and we constantly hold high expectations, this can undermine any positive traits that they possess. Remember to concentrate on the positives, rather than the negatives. When you start to accept your partner, you will be less defensive every time your partner does something to annoy you, and you become more patient as you get to know him or her. This will create change in your relationship as you become more accepting of your partner's little imperfections.

# 29.

## *Letting Go*

You have the skills to make your relationship work. Take the time to invest your energy with your partner, and your effort will pay off in the end. You have to decide yourself if you are in a right relationship, otherwise you need to learn to move on. Moving on can be difficult, especially if you have invested years in the relationship, but you have to find the strength to say that it is not what you are looking for. You are giving yourself and your partner a chance to be happy. It takes a tremendous amount of energy and emotions to stay when it is not working out. You feel miserable. Your partner also can sense it. You need to sit down and discuss where your relationship is heading. Letting go is hard, especially when you feel all alone. It is even harder when you depend on your partner to survive. You need to seek support from your friends and family to get through it. Someone told me how happy he is now that he and his wife are no longer together. When I asked him if it was that bad, he said he felt miserable, but stayed anyway for the sake of their children. It took him ten years to realize he should have left his relationship a long time ago.

# 30.

## *Use A Little Humor*

Relationships are never without its problems. At times, humor can help ease some tensions. You should never take things too seriously, because you are going to get disappointed when things don't go well. Everyone has a different personality, and whether you are an extrovert or an introvert, you can always learn to use humor. Believe me, it lowers your stress levels, and at the end, you learn how to laugh. Have you ever been to a comedy show? People there are laughing and enjoying themselves, and they forget about their daily hassles. In your relationship, learn to be flexible and don't get so uptight about every little detail. If your partner forgets to pick up the cake, don't make a big deal about it. Your partner probably had a busy day and things do slip from time to time. Life is already hard, so try to laugh.

# 31.

## *Being Comfortable*

When you enter a relationship, you tend to find someone who has the same interests, right? This shows that we like to be comfortable with who we are with. However, not every couple shares the same interests. In fact, some differences can be healthy. You need to find a balance in your relationship. Appreciate your partner's hobbies and you may be surprised that you might like them too. If your partner likes to travel and you don't, you have to compromise at times. It is easy to stay in our own comfort zone because change is hard. However, you have to ask yourself if it is doing any good to your relationship. You need to keep in mind that even the most compatible couples can still break up, so don't get tied up to the idea that you have to be completely compatible for the relationship to work. So, be comfortable for who you are. You need to have the confidence to be unique; after all, you are unique. There is nothing more attractive than being you.

# 32.

## *Feeling Guilty*

Don't feel guilty if you break a promise. We like to be perfect in our relationship, but this is not realistic. If you promise you won't yell anymore, every time your partner forgets to call you, you will only be disappointed. Instead, expect that change takes time. As long as you acknowledge your behavior, you will get there. We all have a guilty feeling when we promise something then end up doing the opposite. I think sometimes we have high expectations of ourselves and our partners, and we forget that we make mistakes. It is perfectly fine to relapse once in a while as long as it is not done intentionally. We all need to remember that we are all humans, and human beings make mistakes. The most important thing is when you make a mistake, what are you going to do the next time this happens?

I always get disappointed when I promise something that I don't keep. However, I learned that I was expecting change to occur immediately. When I lessened my expectations and realized it was okay not to be perfect all the time, I did notice the change happening. So, expect that you cannot change yourself overnight, and you will likely get the result you are looking for.

# 33.

## *A Win- Win Situation*

It is tempting to fight in order to win. However, we all feel bad afterwards. You don't have to win to be ahead of the game. Many couples end up blaming the other when they feel their opinions don't count. In order to fight fair, you have to remember that there's another person who is hurt. By fighting fair, you are acknowledging your partner's feelings. You have heard many times how important it is to address the issues, instead of attacking your partner. Every fight begins with an issue, right? So stick to the issue and not at your partner. You need to try to get your point across by using the "I" more than "you." By doing so, it validates your partner's feelings. It is easy to become defensive when we feel we are to blame. It is so important that you try to alleviate this blaming game and remember to fight fair.

We all like to be right, because no one wants to lose. This is just natural. You need to critically think if it is worth your energy or to just let it go sometimes. When emotions run high, this is when you tend to neglect your partner's needs. It is not all about you. There are two people in a relationship, and you have to let go of your selfish needs at times. Also, when couples fight, it is mainly due to disagreements. If your partner likes to golf, then let your partner enjoy his or her hobby as long as he can afford it, and it does not drain your bank account. I believe that if his interest does not hurt anyone, it is best to let this issue go, rather than attacking your partner.

# 34.

## *Break Things Into Smaller Parts*

Many times, you feel overwhelmed about what to do with your relationship. It is easy to just ignore the problems rather than facing it. You need to break things into smaller parts so it does not overwhelm you. Have you ever felt that your day at the office never ends or the household chores never get done? It is the same with your relationship too. If you procrastinate about getting things done, it does get overwhelming. You have the skills to lead your relationship in the right direction. First, you need to start with small goals. Nobody knows you better than yourself. You know what you can manage and what you can't manage. It is easier to start with smaller goals that are manageable, to increase your self-confidence. You need to build your confidence if you want to change or improve your relationship.

# 35.

## *Know What You Can Live With*

Oftentimes, we don't analyze our situation appropriately. We expect things to be perfect. At the end, we end up disappointed. You and your partner need to know what you can live with, depending on your situation. If you feel miserable about your partner's spending habit, then it is obvious that you need to do something about it. However, there are things that probably don't require any actions. Your circumstances are likely to be different than everybody else's situation. So, decide what is best in your situation. When my husband and I built our first home, I knew nothing about homes. I was perfectly okay with the decision that he made. For some, this would have been a problem. You do have to address your concerns with your partner, if you are not comfortable with his or her decision.

# 36.

## *The Blind Spot*

We are our own worst enemy. We normally don't see problems that others may see. Sometimes, it is a blessing in disguise when our close friends or families do point out something in our personal lives. You may miss out on something they are trying to tell you if you take everything they say personally. You have to learn where to draw the line. Most often, people close to you do not want to sabotage your relationships, but rather they want to be helpful. They may not necessarily know what is best for you, but they know you do deserve better. So, when close families offer you advice, it is worth your time that you think it through. If it really does not make sense, thank them for their advice and move on. Have you ever had your parent tell you how to raise your child? Most of you who have children will probably say that this has happened to you. At the time, you probably ignored your parent's advice. As you grow older, you may realize that your parent was just trying to be helpful. My point is that you need to lower your defenses and keep an open mind. Oftentimes, you want to be an expert in your relationship, but it pays to get a second opinion.

# 37.

## *Forgiveness*

It is easy to blame yourself when you make a mistake in your relationship, but it is crucial that you learn to forgive yourself. No matter how difficult your situation is, there is always a solution. It is never a good idea to dwell on your mistakes, much less blame others around you. I have learned that it is far easier to forgive than to hate. When you have so much hate, it creeps up inside you and you feel miserable. When you feel that life is difficult, it helps to understand that nobody has a perfect life. It is up to you to learn to live your life to its fullest. Forgiveness is easier to conquer when you realize that no one is perfect. Parents are great examples when it comes to forgiveness. Oftentimes, they forgive their children no matter what their children have done. In your relationship, you need to learn to forgive when you make a mistake. If your partner does something that you can live with, you also need to forgive him or her.

# 38.

## *There Is Hope*

I learned that I have come a long way to finally say, I have found someone who is right for me. There is always hope in the end of the tunnel. You are going to face many hurdles and at times, you start asking yourself why you can never have a fulfilling life or a relationship. If you just wait until the time is right, you too can get there. You need to remember that only you have the power to change your life or your relationship. It does not come easy. Believe me; I had to learn from my mistakes too. There is always a lesson to learn in life and I hope that you never lose hope. I knew how destructive my relationship was because I felt miserable and unhappy. I had many doubts with my prior relationships, and they were toxic if they had continued. You are no different from someone who has a happy relationship. It is a matter if it is the right one for you. Just remember, you deserve to be happy. You should never fear being alone, if that is what makes you happy. For those who seek love, there's always hope.

# 39.

## *Staying Sane*

Best of all, take care of yourself. When you start to take care of your body, you will feel good about yourself. Every morning, take a fresh air outside or go for a simple walk. It is amazing how simple things can make a difference. As long as you spend a few minutes a day just for yourself, you will notice some changes. If you don't like to exercise, you can try yoga or meditation. When your body starts to change, you too will have the confidence to improve your current relationship or you will have the courage to move on.

You need to take ownership of your past mistakes, and must have the courage to face the future. It is important that you surround yourself with positive people, because they can help you in the right direction. If you feel all alone, you have to try to find that someone who can help you get where you want in your relationship. It is crucial that you don't concentrate too much what you don't have, but you already have. We all feel stuck sometimes and we feel that things will never get better. You have to think outside the box. You have to be creative and stay positive. To stay sane, you have to put perspectives in your life. As I said earlier, you need to reach out to people and always keep in mind that you are not alone. It is important to remember that no one is immune from a failed relationship because we all have experienced it at some point in our life. The difference is how you can move on and learn from it.

# 40.

## *Love Thyself*

The greatest gift you can give to yourself is to love yourself. Never assume things, and love yourself first. It is true that you cannot love somebody until you have loved yourself. It only makes sense. When you have so many doubts about yourself, your perceptions of an ideal relationship are clouded. You need to forgive and forget about what you have done in the past. It really makes life easier when you don't carry that extra baggage with you as you try to move on. We are so preoccupied about pleasing others, but the truth is, you should invest more time in improving yourself. It takes more energy when you are always pleasing others, because it is not who you are. When you accept and love yourself, your life will also change for the better. It is because you don't have to prove yourself to others anymore. You are in control of your life and it only makes sense that you feel good about yourself.

# Helpful Reading:

Brasher, Kimberly. *Toxic Relationships. How to Regain Lost Power In Your Relationship.*
2004. A Better Life Publishing Co.

Carlson, Richard. *Don't Sweat The Small Stuff… and its all small stuff.* 1997. Hyperion.

Forward, Susan. *Toxic Parent.* 1989. Bantam Books.

Galanter, Marc. *Spirituality and The Healthy Mind: Science, Therapy and the Need for*
*Personal Meaning.* 2005. Oxford University Press.

Kane, R. & N. Kane. *From Fear to Love: Overcoming the Barriers to Healthy Relationships.* 2002. Moody.

Kirshenbaum, Mira. *Too Good to Leave; Too Bad to Stay: A Step-By-Step Guide to Help You Decide Whether to Stay In or Get Out of Your Relationship.* 1997. Plume.

Meyer, Ted. *Good Things You Can Learn From a Bad Relationship.* 2004. Santa Monica Press.

To my husband, who has been my biggest supporter and who has helped me be who I am today. To my daughter, Elisa, who is teaching me the value of unconditional love and patience.

## *About the Author:*

Esther Luy received her master's degree in social work at University of Wisconsin-Milwaukee. She resides in Wisconsin with her husband, Neil, who is a practicing internist at an area hospital. She and Neil have a two-year-old daughter.